THERAPY FROM THE HEART OF A
POET, VOL. 2'

THERAPY FROM THE HEART OF A
POET, VOL. 2'

A COLLECTION OF RESTORATIVE, THERAPEUTIC, LOVE – FILLED POEMS!

MONIQUE COONEY-ECHOLS

THERAPY FROM THE HEART OF A POET, VOL. 2'
A COLLECTION OF RESTORATIVE, THERAPEUTIC, LOVE – FILLED POEMS!

iUniverse books may be ordered through booksellers or by contacting:

iUniverse
1663 Liberty Drive
Bloomington, IN 47403
www.iuniverse.com
844-349-9409

Because of the dynamic nature of the Internet, any web addresses or links contained in this book may have changed since publication and may no longer be valid. The views expressed in this work are solely those of the author and do not necessarily reflect the views of the publisher, and the publisher hereby disclaims any responsibility for them.

Any people depicted in stock imagery provided by Getty Images are models, and such images are being used for illustrative purposes only. Certain stock imagery © Getty Images.

Email: Moniqueech@yahoo.com

ISBN: 978-1-6632-4217-4 (sc)
ISBN: 978-1-6632-4218-1 (e)

Print information available on the last page.

iUniverse rev. date: 07/12/2022

CONTENTS

SHORT STORY POEM

ACKNOWLEDGEMENTS

I would like to give praise, glory and honor to my Lord and Savior Jesus Christ. Without him I can do nothing. With him I can do all things. HE IS MY EVERYTHING!

To my daughter Racquel, my son Manuel, and my grandson Jeremiah. Thank you for your love and support. You are my favorite Jewels. Thank you for helping me to shine so effortlessly. I LOVE YOU ALWAYS!

"Therapy From The Heart Of A Poet Vol.2" is a poetic loved-filled tool box that everyone needs…. Created for every being with a pulse and inclination to BECOME, To THRIVE & SUCCEED. For wholeness is the goal and desire in which we ALL need! It's ATTAINABLE for ALL, the words that you're getting ready to consume will have a solidified way of catching you before you fall.

Cheers, to the journey of the climb!
"Therapy From The Heart Of A Poet Vol.2" has everyone of us in mind!

I WANT TO THANK YOU

I want to thank you Lord for carrying me through my darkest time
For giving me peace in my mind
For carrying my heavy load
For embracing me when I had no one else to hold
For giving me rest through every test
For keeping me near to remove all my fear
For being a friend
For showing me that your love never ends
You are my hope when I feel like I can't cope
You are my joy that remains
Even through my darkest pain
So much peace from within
Oh, what joy to be called God's friend
In God I trust, In God I stand
I'm ready to execute my savior's plan!

LIFE PERFECT WIN

If I had the chance to dream again
I would dream of life a perfect win
There would be no cloudy days
Every raindrop would carry bright sun rays
The stars would play my favorite tune
On every tree would be my favorite fruit to consume
The sun would be in just the right spot
There would be no such thing as "Wow it's too hot!"
All the world would wear a smile for day's
As we greet each other along the way
Every heart would be filled with God's joy
Like the moment we received our favorite toy
A time to entertain family and friends
The perfect day that will never end
This would be life's perfect WIN!

HEAVY WINDS

Why do the winds blow so heavily
God has sent His word to fill our bellies
A change has taken place in our atmosphere
This word can only be perceived by those with an ear to hear
As the wind blows, know that God is speaking volume to our souls
I guarantee you, after this wind pass
There will be a word in your belly to last
Oh Earth, open up your ears
Listen while the Lord speaks to all that hear
His word is like a fierce fire
Going forth to Fulfill His every desire!

PROCESS

They tell me I won't feel like this always
That out of this trial will come brighter day's
To hold my head up high
And to not reveal my sigh
Even though this process is trying for me
It's preparing me for who God has created me to be
So, I tell myself to be still
To stay centered in God's will
I want to fulfill everything you require of me
To show you everything you desire to see
Oh, how my soul travails
While my heart yearns to do well
I look to you for my expected end
You are my God, and a true friend!

THE JOY OF LAUGHTER

The Joy of Laughter
The way to heal from life disasters
The place that bubbles over from within
Flowing outward into a joyous grin
The sound that rings with great delight
Filled with amusement for your darkest night
The Joy of Laughter
Setting the mood for whatever comes after
It's music for the heart and soul
The medicine with a holistic goal
A chuckle with a breath of fresh air
Repeating itself without a care
The Joy of Laughter
Let this laughter carry you into your most profound breakthrough
While leading and guiding you to your inner truth!

REBUKE THE STORM

If He rebuked the storm in the Sea
Surly He will rebuke the storm in me
There has been enough wind for this rainy day
Watch my God calm the storm that's in my way
I have the faith of a mustard seed
That grows far beyond all that anyone can believe
Eyes have not seen, ears have not heard
The benefits of trusting in God's Word
Faith that carries me through every storm
Trusting you has become a part of my norm
This battle is not mine alone
This battle is for He that sits on the throne!

GREAT THINGS

You have something planned for me
You have something great for my eyes to see
My way and Path are bright
Filled with your amazing light
The plans you have for me, will lead me straight into my destiny
Giving me a hope that will never make me ashamed
What great peace when I trust in your name
You have an awesome plan
One that can only be executed by your hands
Oh, the Joy that resonates in me
When I think about the quest to becoming who you've called me to be
A future filled with many great things
A glorious promise of what the eyes have not seen!

LIGHT

The God that gives light to the world
To every man, woman, boy and girl
A light for all to see
Leaving hope for every generation after me
Thank you for shining so bright on us
A hope filled with life that we can all trust!

MORNING KISS

Every morning when I wake up, I blow you a kiss
To the God I love so dear, I've found a way to keep you near
I will never let you go far from me
You are the God who controls my destiny
My love for you is far beyond compare
This space in my heart is only for you to share!

COUNT IT ALL JOY

Count it all Joy when you can't see your way
And all your clouds are dark and gray
Count it all Joy when the enemy comes in like a flood
And your whole life feels misunderstood
Remember this season will not last for long
We have a miracle working God sitting on the throne
A righteous man may fall seven times, but we'll watch him rise again
With the promise of His word, we are guaranteed to WIN!

OUR KING

There is only one that can give light in darkness
Life to a dead thing
He is our resurrected King
The God that holds our hand
As we commit to His plan
Making this course light to run
As we look to His only Son
His Kingdom has all things
All the necessities life can bring!

WINDOW CRACK

There is a crack in my window
And every time the wind blows
I hear the sound of a whistle
It whispers to me… "You are not alone, listen to my sweet tone"
As the wind blows, and the tree leaves shake
This sound simply states
"You are not alone, listen to my sweet tone"
What a lovely tune it plays
As I stand here in total amaze
I've found a cleaver way to use my hands
Each clap mimics the sound of a band
"Clap!" "Clap!" "Boom!" "Boom!"
Both hands coming together as one
Beating like the sound of a drum
Then I open my eyes to see
What is this Euphonious sound that whispers back to me
Such beautiful leaves tapping against my window
Making an amazing sound every time the wind blows!

CAREFUL HEART

When someone breaks your heart
The heart breaker should share your pain
Maybe then, it won't leave such a great stain
I feel this is only fair
When someone handles your heart without care
The heart is a place where all the fun times are stored
And all your favorite moments are on record
Handle other's heart with care
Help fill them with fond memories to share
Do unto others as you will have life do unto you
And watch the promises of God hold true!

IMAGINATION WITHOUT LIMIT

I am guilty of all that I see
A dream I hope to make a reality
When I close my eye's marvelous thoughts appear
Thoughts of a beautiful atmosphere
My mind is given to total creativity
And manifesting all that is within me
You said "Let us make man in our image"
With an imagination without limit
Let us take them to a place they have never been before
A way to receive everything they have in store
Go make all your dreams a reality
And build all that your imagination can see!

HIDDEN IN YOU

My favorite place to be
Is under the shadow of the Almighty
A place where His protection power flow
And my faith began to grow
The secret place of the Most High
The place where He always hear my cry
The place where His shadow covers me
And His reflection is what everyone sees
Jehovah-Nissi, my life is hidden in you
The place where your love shields through and through!

SECOND CHANCE

What is life without a chance to love again
What is life without a second win
I'll share with you all that's dear to me
In hopes that this time our love will be
Will this second journey be my best?
And bring my heart to a place of rest
Will our love push away every stone
And leave us open before His throne
Lord, thank you for a new heart to love again
A heart full of hope, where true love always WIN!

UNWIND

Carry your thoughts to a place without time
Give your mind space to unwind
Concentrate on what's pure and true
Allow this moment to carry you through
Let the mind of Christ rein
It will remove all your hidden pain!

RACE

Great is thy Mercy
So amazing is thy Grace
Your unmerited favor keeps us all in this race
Show me my good parts
So that I will have a head start
This race I am sure to win
With a God who knows my beginning and the end.

THE CARES OF THIS WORLD

I will not carry the cares of this world
For they are not mine to bare
So, I cast all my cares to the one who is always there
The one who floods my soul
Whenever life problems get to heavy to hold
He that takes all my broken pieces
And uses them like I never had a weakness
There is no match for His mighty hand
All fall at His great command
He brings Joy to my sorrow
He tells me to take no thought for tomorrow
Your tomorrow is a day already written in stone
Every prayer you've prayed, has already reached His throne
So, don't fret about the cares of this life
You have everything you need in Christ!

CHEERFUL GIVER

Oh, how I love a cheerful giver!
One who deeds are a Joy to remember
One who's bosom is full of reward
One who's claims every blessing stored
One who moves with great expectancy
A perfect picture of the word Prosperity
The one who brings overflow in every way
I am your giver, the one who will always repay
Show them how loud you can cheer!
Let them see the reflection of a changed atmosphere
Oh, how I love a cheerful giver!
One who's deeds are a Joy to remember
Paint a picture for all to see
The blessings and reward of walking with me!

THE SECRET PLACE

There is a place made manifest to man
A place where only the righteous stand
A place for all to pursue
What a special place I've found in you
The secret place of the Most High
The one who's shadow covers like the sky
It has always been your plan to be one with man
So here in our secret place I stand
The place where I call truce with myself
And depend solely on you and no one else!

REWARD

Time to gather the wheat from your harvest
God has made His face to shine on all of us
Time to gather from every seed sown
There will be no place His name is not known
He is the God that is more than enough
Come! Claim your reward of a full cup
A fountain that never ends
This is an eternal flow… you will never thirst again!

DENTED CAN

Of all the cans that the store manager scanned
Why was there a dent in my can?
Of all the cans upon the shelf
This one reminds me of myself
Standing all alone...
It was plain to see, why it was the last can waiting just for me
It had its own unique quality
Solid... And full of substance!
Waiting for someone to trust it
Ready to fulfill someone's need
What an honor to be used as a tool to feed!

ROSEMARY BLEND

Let me take you to a place you've never been
Where the aroma is Rosemary Blend
Where all the land is filled with Daisies
And the Lilies dance is so amazing
The trees stand out like a lit candles wick
Each one creating its own magic trick
Where the birds fly South, and are not seen as before
While the Squires run out with a hand full of nuts to store
Every fruit tree is planted just right
Every fruit it bears is sweet and ripe
This must be the Land of the Canaanites!

PATH

I want to stand where no one has stood before
And discover new revelations through every door
I want to create a path for the whole world to repeat
A path with only your face to seek
Open a door that no man has seen before
Wide enough for all to explore
To proclaim your name boldly in all the Earth!
What priceless value, what great worth!

THE WAIT

I don't know how long it may take
But I know a God who makes no mistakes
My days ahead are much better than these
I have many promises I've yet to receive
I count it all Joy in this present state
Only the strong heart can endure this wait
Let patience have her perfect stand
Let her give hope to the inner man
Let wisdom reveal what is best
And help us to endure every test!

GREATER THINGS THAN THESE

Greater things than these I expect to receive
I am the child of a King
My eyes have not seen, nor my ears heard
All the things we have because we trust God's word!
My God can never fail
He stands on His word, He makes all things well
So many things are working for my good
I would praise Him with ten thousand tongues if I could
That still would not be enough
To give praise and honor to the God I love to trust
My hope in God will always remain
He promised me a hope that won't make me ashamed
There are greater things than these, if you could only believe!

MY UNCONDITIONAL LOVE

My Child to love you unconditionally
Is my way of helping your soul to stay free
To give you your own free will
Gives you a greater life to fulfil
I am your God… I love who you are
You are my creation, my true star
I love you unconditionally
There is nothing that can separate you from me
You will always be enough
Nothing can stop our fellowship and trust
My unconditional Love!

GIFT

Was this gift always there?
Maybe it was, and I was not aware
Did it come from my hidden place
You know, my God ordained space
This feeling I hold so dear, is taking me into my atmosphere
The place I was chosen to dwell
Taking me to a place I know so well
This atmosphere is full of authenticity
A space created just for me
A chance to walk in what I like
A chance to bring my dreams to life!
Holding on to my moment of truth
Ready to serve the world with my gift from you!

NO GREATER LOVE

There is no greater love than this
A love that gives me everything in life I missed
So much Joy, I can't explain
This Joy covers all of my pain
There is no greater love than this
Your love never puts my heart at risk
Today I give you all of me
In exchange for a life, I long to see
Great are all of your plans
They give directions like only a true father can
A path that takes me through life chapters
With great hope, for the morning after!

ABOVE CALAMITY

Lord, take me to a place that's higher than me
A place to rise above all calamity
I want to hold my head up high again
And soar like an Eagle through the wind
I want to enter that place of tranquility
To create an atmosphere of peace for me
I don't want to carry this load anymore
I'm going to trust that your word will lead me to my open door
Please remove this heavy weight
And give me the strength I need to endure this wait!

AMAZING GOD

When life carries you to those places you just don't understand
The places that feel unknown to man
"He is still an amazing God"
When that door doesn't open for you
And you watch someone else walk through
"He is still an amazing God"
When we have our own plans
And they crumble in the palm of our hands
"He is still an amazing God"
When we know we should totally rely upon you
But we turn to someone else to get through
Against all odds… You stand as an Amazing God!

HIS THOUGHTS OF YOU

I know my thoughts of you
You are my tried and true
The one that carry my name
The one that bear the cross without shame
I know my thoughts of you
You are the one that is perfectly made
The one I called good on the sixth day
The one that desires my will
And walk in all that my word reveals
I know my thoughts of you
The one my son set free
And he did it all in complete humility
You are the one who call on the Most-High God
Whenever there is a problem to solve
The one who is wonderfully made
With a power that will never fade
You are my eternal child
The one who pass every test and trial
My thoughts of you are pure and true
I give you hope and a promise to pursue
All my promises are yes and amen
To give you an expected plan!

ALL WINNING

You never forget your daughter
I am the one you called into divine order
You've changed every part of me
Turning me into someone I am proud to be
"I can do all things!" There are no impossible dreams!
All my doors have new beginnings
Look at me! I'm all winning!

OPEN DOOR

There was no thought of a brighter day
All my dreams seemed so far away
All my fears felt impossible to face
I carried every weight and pain
So much until my heart felt strained
I thought I'd seen everything life had in store
Then came my open door!
So many beautiful things
Things I never thought life would bring
A God that was always there
Filled my bosom with love and care
Causing my cup to overflow
Giving increase to every seed I sow!

LAND OF MILK AND HONEY

God is going to do great things
Our God is setting the scene
He has not abandoned you
His great power will carry you through
This story has you in mind
With the God that transcends time
Many blessings He has in store
He is like no other you've seen before
Taking you into the land of Milk and Honey
Commanding the wicked to release all your money
Pouring out His spirit on all flesh
Giving us the strength to pass every test
Filling us with power, like only our God can
What great Joy! He has given us the Land!

MORNING MEDITATION

You are my morning meditation
The one I seek without hesitation
My thoughts swarm to you
The God I love to pursue
The one my eyes are fastened upon
Making this a Royal race to run
You are my King from on high
The God of love, with an unlimited supply!

ORIGINAL MAN

The original man
Made from God's plan
With the original gene
That produces every human being
That strong Melanin!
That makes us unique from them all
That dark skin with a Mocha blend
This is what makes the whole world Kin!

A WISH

I wish dreams were made from stars
There would be dreams everywhere you are
The kind that travels through space and time
A dream to dazzle all man kind
It will carry everyone's heart desire
Full of a hope that is sure to inspire!

A KISS

Here is a kiss in your direction
A kiss to show my deepest affection
This special kiss is all for you
To help you through all you do
And if by chance your whole life change
Here's a kiss for my love to remain!

REMOVABLE STAIN

Your Joy remains in me
Your peace sustains me
I offer myself to you
With full knowledge of the world pleasures in view
Everything I have is yours
Because of you my faith has been restored
The God my heart loves to pursue
My life has new meaning ever since I've found you
If anyone ask me… What do I recommend for the stain of sin?
I would tell them the blood of Jesus my friend
He said… Go your way and sin no more
I set before you an open door
To make sure your sin stain doesn't remain
Just call upon my Savior's name!

REMAIN STILL

As I sit here on your Potter's wheel
Waiting for your plan to be revealed
Waiting for your word to take effect
Knowing that my time is not yet
Help me to remain still, as I sit here on your Potter's wheel
Give me the patience I need
So that I may be a vessel made to please
And if I am not pleasing to you, make me over again
Until your Potter's wheel has taken its last spin!

ALWAYS HERE

Though my eyes can't see your plan for me
I yield my heart in complete humility
Every part of me I yield to you
Watch as this building stand on truth
You carry me through every trial and test
Because of you, I will always give my best
You're always here for me whenever my sight gets to deem to see
What a mighty God we serve, taken time to shield and preserve
When I can't see, you are my way
Thank you, Lord… for bringing me to a brighter day
Love without end, peace that forever transcends
Every hurdle, every obstacle
Your peace is like nothing I've ever felt before!

GOD'S PLAN

I have ordained you to carry out my plan
Your purpose goes beyond the knowledge of man
I've ordered your steps and given you a guide
Carry him always by your side
The Holy Spirit is your compass while walking through
Always take him with you
There will be no weariness during your quest
Just trust in me for divine rest
Your path is laid out in pure gold
Your feet are anointed from the very sole
Walk in your purpose, I'll make it plain to see
Set your eyes on the mark and follow me
I am your future, I have your plan
I designed every purpose before it was ever given to man!

WHO?

Who made the Heavens and the Earth?
Who replenish the trees when they thirst?
Travel through space and time
While inhabiting mankind
Balancing the winds with His scale
Making sure that all is well
Giving light at just the right time
Shining a hope that is divine
He who gave His only Son
To ensure all my battles are won
You are the God who is second to none!

EXPRESSION

Give me a poem that will reach me when I'm down
Give me a song that will keep me when no one else is around
Give me a word that will revive my soul
Give me your touch when I need someone to hold
Give me strength to carry out your plan
Make my life an expression of your greatest command!

DESERVED PRAISE

Thank you, Jesus for healing my body and making me whole
Thank you for the Joy down in my soul
For bringing me out with a new shout!
For all of my wins, and giving me life without end
What a great God I serve
What great praise you deserve
A praise without limit
Ten thousand tongues could only begin it
My praise will last forever
What intriguing times we'll have together!

BESTOWED BLESSINGS

I want to thank the Lord for all the blessings He has bestowed on me
He has lifted my head far above my enemy
He has placed my feet on solid ground
He's turned my whole life around
He has given me Vineyards I didn't plant
He has caused me to triumph over every attack
He has given me a roof over my head, food, and a warm bed
God has supplied all my needs
He's given me His great love to succeed.

BEYOND THE VEIL

For all who wonder what happens beyond the veil
This is where you wish your past life farewell
A place provided for the life of a King
No hokes, pranks or imaginary things
Where every desire is made from the heart
Where everyone can have a brand-new start
For all who wonder what happens beyond the veil
This is where the Holy Spirit dwells
Where all your prayers are heard
And a special seat is reserved.

FAITH IN YOU

My God I yield my all to you
In hope to build a life of truth
You've changed my life in every way
In hope to build a life of faith
Tearing down walls that I thought would never fall
Remaining in you, I conquered all
There is nothing I can't do
As long as I keep my faith in you
Thank you for never leaving me
And placing no limits on all I can be!

HIS WILL

A man with a mind stayed on Christ
Is a man that makes good choices throughout life
There is nothing that will take you further, than the divine will of the Father
Giving Him your life to lead, is the only true way to succeed
There is nothing greater for you, than the path God has given you to pursue
God has great things to reveal, if we would only choose His will!

GRATEFUL

I Thank God for shining His light on the dark places inside of me
Through every test you've given me victory
Thank you for writing my name in the Lambs book of life
And making it an honor to carry your light
For every moment I've called out your name
For not allowing hope to leave me ashamed
For holding my hand through it all
For catching me before every fall
For teaching me to walk in your truth
For giving me favor whenever the enemy tried to pursue
For every battle I've fought, I gained another level
Declaring total victory over the devil!

WATCH THE BEE'S SWARM

No need to wonder who's side I am on
Just watch the way the Bee's swarm
Like the Honey that is just right
So is this season of great delight
In this season I am at a steady pace
Like a sprint runner who's won first place!

THANKSGIVING

Thanksgiving, one of my favorite times of the year
A time for lots of fun and family cheer
A time to thank God for all He has done
While sharing this day with love one's!

WHAT IS RIGHT FOR ME

God knows what is right for me
Even when my eyes can't see
He carries me to a safe place
That place where our Spirits embrace
He shows me what is right for me
And gives me new victory!

REVEAL

I will reveal everything to you
And withhold nothing
I will hide my deepest secrets in you
And trust no other
You are my rock, my strong place
My rescue from life storms
You renew my mind, and keep me calm
My spirit is refreshed, like a bright spring day after the rain
I require counsel from no other
Your Word feed my soul
Your Word is a light that chases away all darkness
Your Word patterns the course of my life!

IMAGE OF MYSELF

The greatest love of all is inside of me
That helps me to become everything I was ordained to be
Producing a great image of myself, will help me attain my God given wealth
I will obtain all that He has for me
To duplicate the image of what my Creator sees
Spirit of God help me to manifest every gift within myself
Your divine direction will keep me from becoming someone else!

MORE THAN ENOUGH

I am the God who is more than enough
The God you can trust
I'm the one to make your loads light
I'll carry you through your night
Don't worry, take no thought for your tomorrow
I will bear your sorrows
What great things our God will do
What a gracious God who has chosen you
To represent His only Son
To show us the way true victory is won!

TRUE WOMEN OF VIRTUE

To the women I've watched throughout my life
Thank you for the strength you've shown through your walk with Christ
Watching you has given me courage that is beyond compare
What great things have happened all because YOU were there
God's wisdom flows from you, as you declare to the world His Word is true
You teach me to hold my head high, and with all tenacity, reach for the sky!
Like the waters of a spring, and the beauty of a Rose, your love and kindness
continually flow
Oh, what great things God has prepared for you!
A woman who walks in such grace and truth!
Don't ever change who you are
Your humble ways are the best by far
Yes, we are watching you!
An anointed Woman of God in full view!

HOLY PLACE

That secret place where I go with you, that place no one else has access to
That Holy place in me, that place of true serenity
A place where we both dwell, my place of "All Is Well"
A place reserved just for you, and your Holy Spirit of Truth
Reminding me of who I am
An anointed child of the great "I AM"
Thank you for our secret place
That place the world nor time can ever erase!

CREATE IN ME

Create in me a new thing
Something to devote my time to
Something for my hands to pursue
Something to make you proud
That show the world that I am your child
This praise belongs to only you
There is no other I will give the glory to
Perfect your will in me
Flaunt all the things you desire to see
The beginning of a new thing
A way to manifest all my dreams!

DAD

To lose a father no matter how old you are
Is one of the greatest trials by far
So many memories that make my heart smile
To meditate on each of them will surely take a while
You have filled my heart with so much Joy, so many special thoughts of you
I will cherish them forever
Dad, your love will leave me NEVER
To have a heart like yours is a rare treasure to find
All your acts of endless love, you're definitely one of a kind
A Provider, A Protector, A Giver, just to name a few
This list goes on and on as I reminisce of you
Your bold humor never takes us by surprise
It's that unique laugh you share that gives us all that special feeling inside
Choosing others care above your own
This is something only a special heart could have shown
Never asking for anything in return
You stayed strong in the faith as you ran your race
You gave all the praise to God
Knowing that with God and family, life would not seem as hard
A wise man you were, who never hesitated to smile
You are a fine representation of a Father, and example for every Child!

A GRATEFUL PLACE

I'm so grateful to be here
Because for some, this day never appeared
I'm so Grateful to still have my peace
Because someone troubles have yet to cease
I'm so grateful to still be standing strong
Because many others couldn't stand for very long
I'm so grateful to wear a smile
Because someone couldn't make it through their trial
I'm so grateful to have total trust in you
Because not everyone has chosen to
I'm so grateful that you are my God
Because with you nothing is too hard!

SLEEPWALKING

I wish I could dream a dream that kept me awake
There would be no limit to the roads I would take
I would walk the Road of Success, and settle for nothing less
I would take the Road of Gratitude, this would be my continuous mood
I would keep straight onto the Road of Faith
This road will secure my win in every race
Turn right onto Purpose Road, to confirm every dream I've ever told
Travel the Road of Elevation, and climb the mountain of great Salvation
I would take the stairway to my open door
And embrace every blessing God has in store
And when I awake from my sleep
I will find that all my Quests are complete!

UNIQUE MISSION

Don't take your life's journey, and later find out it was all a phony
You travel all the way through, just to find out this was not the real you
All because you didn't pursue the one who really loves you
The Maker knows his creation. He is the one that formed the Nations
The one who spoke our whole life into existence
He has given you a unique mission
Don't let the man in the mirror, show you a false generated figure
I have hope in this one thing
For all to become a unique vessel for the King!

LOW PLACE

All I have left is a dream
Everything else has been wiped clean
There is only one place to turn
That is to the God that I yearn
Help me to rise from this low place
I feel like my whole life is being erased
Everything I have, I will lose
If you don't show me the right path to choose
I know I'm not in this by myself
I hope that this season is leading me into my wealth
My faith is everything to me
Without It I have no vision to see
So, I hold on tight to my belief
As I pray for the blessings to be released
My hope is in the God of my Salvation
Please deliver me from my present situation!

BRIGHT PATH

Show me the path you have laid for me
That place my eyes are anointed to see
Don't let my soul go astray
There is no peace in wondering from day to day
Please give my mind the rest it need
This is the only way I can proceed
Assure my path is bright for me
And lead me to a sure Victory!

THE TRUE YOU

I love the place that I'm in
It's so comfortable in my own skin
No way I would want to be you
And miss the chance to be true!

HERO

You are my everything God
I love you more than anything
You are my life line
You carry me through my hard times
You are the very air I breath
You are everything I need
You cover me both day and night
You are my Hero by right!

FUTURE HUSBAND

Dear Future Husband
I can't wait to hold you in my arms
To release my most hidden charm
To carry you in my heart forever
Your spirit will leave me, Never
The very essence of you
Gives my life a whole new view
Come share with me life moments
Let's take this world like we own it
It will always be You and I
We will break the mold in whatever we try
Standing side by side
What a safe place for us to reside
Two becoming one?
What a complicated equation for some
But we will show proof of it all!
Our God has anointed us for the long haul!

SHARE A MOMENT

The Joy of the Lord is my strength!
I will wear a smile always
And spread my Joy in everyway
I will share my special moments with you
You can always lean on me to help you through!

STAND

God, sometimes my circumstance makes me feel like I can't make it
But your word offers me hope, so it won't feel like I can't take it
So, I take a stand against the enemy!
I stand by faith, because I am sold out to this race
Knowing that in time I will have my win
My trust in you will never end!

OUR WORLD

Lord, how can we rest when our world is in such great distress?
How do we remain sane when the world is in so much pain?
How can we remain strong? When we feel so all alone.
So, we hold on tight to your hand.
We know that you always have a plan.
We may not understand everything.
But we know you will bring us out on Eagles wings!
We will soar like never before!
Because of the God we all adore!

AFFLICTION

Lord, as you carry me through this trying time
Give me your peace to ease my mind
As I go through this affliction
Give me what I need to overcome this condition
Where I am weak, I ask for your strength to stand strong
I know I'm not in this battle alone
Your Spirit will cover me, like a blanket of tranquility
I stand sure knowing that I am always on your mind
Give me victory in this trying time
As I hold on to my faith
Assure me that I've already won this race!

HAPPY NAPPY HAIR

I know I'm cute
Even if you can't get with the styles of my roots
Wearing my hair kinky and nappy
This is a sure sign that I am happy
Happy with who I am!
And I won't hesitate to mention
How my hair draws such a crowd of attention
So, go ahead wear your hair fine
But don't look down on mine
This hair is inherited from a powerful nation
The first look of the original creation
Oh…how you admire my woven weave
Wishing you could get the strings of your hair to cleave
This beauty is from a look you could only imagine
With styles created from all kinds of patterns
This hair is the best by far!
It can't be imitated or produced from a jar
The hair that comes with many shades of skin
Light and dark brown, with a Mocha spin
Oh…what beauty radiates when I walk
My words are strong and assertive when I talk
Please don't fear my flamboyant gear
Things aren't always the way they appear
This hair does not define me
But it will sure leave a lasting impression behind me
It's all apart of my eccentric nature
Making me unique from every creature!

ALL I NEED

God, when I think about you are all I need
I don't have to worry anymore about how to succeed
Having you in my life is more than enough
In you God, I put my trust
You are my greatest treasure
You make every part of my life better
When I thought my life was falling apart at the seams
You showed me that I can live beyond my dreams
Yes, you are all I need
Special times with you makes it easy for me to believe
Your Word is life!
What an honor to be joint heirs with Christ!

COME SEE A MAN

When she moved the whole world moved with her
No one had a reason to stand still
Her light radiates with a Solar appeal
Masking her sorrows was a thing of the past
This was a God thing that was meant to last
Come see a man!
Who has the whole world in His hand
He told me all things I did not know
He showed me the way to life eternal
Come see a man!
Who holds the keys to the Masters plan
He'll tell you all things about yourself
You will never put your trust in anyone else!

UNLIMITED LOVE

I want to be able to love without limit
That can never happen in my life without you in it
Please don't ever leave my side
In you is where I will always reside
Knowing your love is always there
Give's my heart unlimited care
So, I stop to rest in you
Knowing there is no limit to what true love will do!

HEAVY LOAD

Great is thy Mercy
Amazing is thy Grace
Thank you for the strength and courage to make it through another day
Another hill to climb, another road to cross
Thank you for the power and courage to deal with this loss
What a heavy load of grief it holds
This cry is coming from my very soul
Heal me with your touch
This suffering Is beginning to be too much
This moment of fear is weighing on me, as if that day was still here
God restore my soul, and make me whole
This is not a battle I chose
God, you are the head of all things
Saturate me with a love nothing can come between
The love you give will carry me completely through
My difficult times are lighter all because of you!

GOD'S PATH

There is a path that seems right unto man
However, do not mistake this for God's plan
God's path is paved in gold
With all the beauty your eyes can behold
On this path where the Angels sing with their voices on high
While praise and worship fill the sky!
There is a path that seems right unto man
So, please be careful, and chose the Master's plan
Your path may have everything your heart desires
But, is it really what God requires?

A KINGS CHILD

A Kings child never has to worry
We all know the end of their story
For it is already written
The devil knows he is already smitten
A story of complete victory!
Enough to create a new era in history
One that reflects a Kings child
A child anointed for every trial
One with plans of an expected end
God has prepared his child a mountain of GREAT WINS!

GOD PROVIDES

May the sun dry all your tears
May the moon calm your fears
May the night cover your sadness
May the morning bring you gladness
May the rain saturate you within
May the thunder cast out all sin
May the wind bring you a breath of hope
May the stars give you a broader scope
May the flowers give you another Rose to smell
May the tree's dance reveal that "All is well"
May the grass teach you there is always room to grow
May the mountains give you their greatest show
No matter what life brings
May God provide the answer to all things

SHORT STORY POEM

{HALF PAST NINE}

PART I

This is the story of my life. The day I chose my wife. These words were running through my mind "What if I ran out of time?" as I looked up at the clock with the number nine. I had just awoken from a deep sleep. One that felt like I was out for weeks. As soon as the phone rang, then started the moment of my pain. The news I heard that day, would change my life in every way.

I have your wife here with me, and only a large ransom can set her free. The time is very short. So, meet me at the South-Central Basketball Court. Bring with you all your valuables, and everything you deem salvageable. "This cannot be happening to me! I can't imagine life without my wife beside me!" So, I headed to the South- Central Basketball Court. Wearing only a pair of red shorts. With every piece of Jewel, I owned in my hand, trying to think of an escape plan.

"Where is this beauty of mine?" Looking at the clock, it was half past Nine. Hey you! Come here! "Here I am...Where is my wife! As I yelled out without thinking twice. I have every piece of Jewel I own in my hand. So, please stick to the plan! Let my wife go! Give her back to me! You promised you'd set her free!" She is not yours alone, said a voice as shrewd as can be. You are not the only one with a ransom for me.

Over there is the car next to that tree, is another man who say's she is his wife to be. And he also has money for me.

"What are you saying? Where is my wife!" Calm down Sir, if you value your life! What do you know about the woman you hold so dear? I heard you met her drunk over a can of Beer. "Yes, it was a can of Beer. But that is not why I am here! Give me my wife! I won't say it twice!"

Your wife is over here, right next to me. Throw me your valuables and get down on your knees. "I'm right here kneeling down before you. So, please carry your promise through. I need to see her face, show me that she is safe!" I will release her at the right time. Until then, she is mine!

PART II

I have told your husband to come, and boy is he dumb! He hasn't a clue who he is married to. Your other man is right over there. And yet he still doesn't care. He continually yells "Where is my wife!" without thinking twice. It must be nice to be loved by two. Let's see which one you will choose. One of them has got to go. Maybe then you can be faithful! This is all your fault. I bet you thought you would never get caught. Walking around like you don't have a care in the world. While they both thought you were their only girl. While the whole time, this was not true. Oh, my is she playing the both of you!

Hey! Your wife is right here! Come closer, you don't have to fear. I know this whole thing looks like a big mess. But trust me when I say this is your wife's test. She has a choice. It's you, or the guy in the Rolls Royce. She needs to make up her mind. It is now half past Nine. She meets him here every Thursday night. She makes sure there is no one else in sight. But I can see both of them from afar. Every Thursday I wonder where you are.

She holds his hand, while they make all sorts of plans. I watch them kiss, as if you don't exist! So, here is your chance to settle the score. You don't have to see them together anymore. Just walk over to that car, and let him know who you are. Tell him she is your wife! And for what he has done there is a price! Tell him to open the car door, and give him to the count of four. Then grab him from behind. Let him know he is out of time!

He will not meet with your wife anymore. This is where you even the score! Take that weapon you brought with you, and use it on the one's who are untrue! Go! Your wife is safe here. Go! You don't have to fear! This is his last time ruining someone else life. He is the same man that stole my wife! Now he is at it again. Only this time he will not win! I am giving you the chance I did not take. Now my wife is gone, and it is too late!

PART III

{Wife} Stop! Hunny, please do not go! This is not the answer we are looking for. This will all end very bad. Don't make the wrong choice all because you are mad. We will get through this together. There is no storm we can't weather. I love you with all my heart. Please let's make a new start. There is nothing we can't get through. Let me show you, my love is true. I don't care anything about the man in the Rolls Royce. Hunny, please make the right choice. "How will I know this adulteress relationship will end? You are my wife, and my best friend." {Wife} Hunny, our love will stand the test of time. Remember I am yours, and you are mine.

Don't listen to her! Go! Take care of it, he is over there. Kill him while he is unaware! "No! I can't do it! Please give me back my wife, so we can work through this. I'm sorry for what happened between him and your wife. But that's no reason to ruin my life. Killing him will not bring your wife back. This is not the sensible way to act. Whatever him and your wife did, must have been very cruel. But don't let the enemy use you as his tool! Every man will reap what he has sowed. It's God's choice to decide when each of us should go. Give your heart to Christ, and He will give you a new life. A chance to start over again. Come… let us pray my friend!"

THE END

Printed in the United States
by Baker & Taylor Publisher Services